Eat Your Colors

White Food Fun

by Lisa Bullard

Capstone press

Mankato, Minnesota

A+ Books are published by Capstone Press,
151 Good Counsel Drive, P.O. Box 669, Mankato, Minnesota 56002.
www.capstonepress.com

Library of Congress Cataloging-in-Publication Data
Bullard, Lisa.
    White food fun / by Lisa Bullard.
    p. cm.—(A+ books. Eat your colors)
    Includes bibliographical references and index.
    ISBN-13: 978-0-7368-5384-2 (hardcover)
    ISBN-10: 0-7368-5384-7 (hardcover)
    1. Food—Juvenile literature. 2. White—Juvenile literature. I. Title. II. Series.
TX355.B92885 2006
641.3—dc22   2005026663

Summary: Brief text and colorful photos describe common foods that are the color white.

Credits

Donald Lemke, editor; Kia Adams, designer; Kelly Garvin, photo researcher

Photo Credits

All photos by Capstone Press/Karon Dubke except pages 18–19 by Getty Images Inc./Aura

Note to Parents, Teachers, and Librarians

This Eat Your Colors book uses full-color photographs and a nonfiction format to introduce children to the color white. *White Food Fun* is designed to be read aloud to a pre-reader or to be read independently by an early reader. Photographs help listeners and early readers understand the text and concepts discussed. The book encourages further learning by including the following sections: Recipe, Glossary, Read More, Internet Sites, and Index. Early readers may need assistance using these features.

Table of Contents

Tasty White

Gooey, crunchy, salty, and sweet. White foods can make your mouth water. What is your favorite white food?

Frothy, white milk bubbles, tickle your nose. Drink the whole glass. It's good for your bones.

Do you know what the white part of an egg is called? An egg white! The yellow center is the yolk.

Pop! Pop! Pop! When kernels of popcorn are heated, they explode. Their insides become delicious white outsides!

White Veggies

Cauliflower is a cousin
of broccoli. It looks like a
big white flower.

Small, white mushrooms with round tops are called buttons. Many other kinds of mushrooms grow in different shapes and sizes.

Stinky White Foods

Phew! Fresh garlic bulbs can stink up a room. But a tiny bit adds big flavor to food.

White onions are so stinky they can bring tears to your eyes. But their flavor in food can make you smile.

Sweet White Treats

Marshmallows taste great in hot chocolate. Their gooey white sweetness melts in your mug.

Tap, tap, tap. Coconut shells
are hard to crack. The white
fruit inside is called meat. Its
sweet taste is worth the wait!

Ice cream comes in many flavors and almost every color. But America's number one favorite is white vanilla.

Blow out the candles, and grab a great big piece. A creamy, white cake makes any birthday sweet! Aren't white foods fun to eat?

South Pole Sundae

For a special occasion, try this sweet treat. It's as cold and white as the South Pole!

What You Will Need

Ice cream scoop

Vanilla ice cream

Bowl and spoon

Coconut shavings

Whipped cream

Mini marshmallows

Cherries

How to Make a South Pole Sundae

1. Scoop vanilla ice cream into a bowl.

2. Sprinkle on your choice of white toppings.

3. Top the South Pole Sundae with whipped cream and a red cherry.

4. Imagine you are a polar explorer who has planted a red flag at the top of a snow pile. Dig through the sweet white sundae in your bowl.

5. Don't eat too fast or you'll get brain freeze!

Glossary

broccoli (BROK-uh-lee)—a green vegetable with rounded heads on stalks

bulb (BUHLB)—the onion-shaped underground plant part from which some plants grow; the bulb of a garlic plant adds flavor to food.

cousin (KUZH-uhn)—a member of the same vegetable family

frothy (FRAW-thee)—having lots of small bubbles

kernel (KUR-nuhl)—a grain or seed of corn, wheat, or other cereal plant

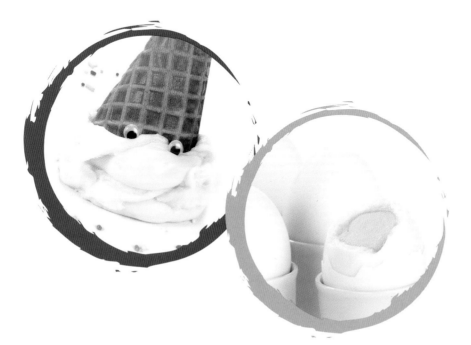

Read More

Dahl, Michael. *White: Seeing White All Around Us.* Colors. Mankato, Minn.: Capstone Press, 2005.

Whitehouse, Patricia. *White Foods.* The Colors We Eat. Chicago: Heinemann, 2002.

Internet Sites

FactHound offers a safe, fun way to find Internet sites related to this book. All of the sites on FactHound have been researched by our staff.

Here's how:

1. Visit *www.facthound.com*

2. Type in this special code **0736853847** for age-appropriate sites. Or enter a search word related to this book for a more general search.

3. Click on the **Fetch It** button.

FactHound will fetch the best sites for you!

Index